Wine is good for you

A comical collection of quotes for wine aficionados

ISBN: 978-1-912155-58-3

Created by Reckless Indiscretions
Images under license from Shutterstock

BELL & MACKENZIE
PUBLISHING LIMITED
www.bellmackenzie.com

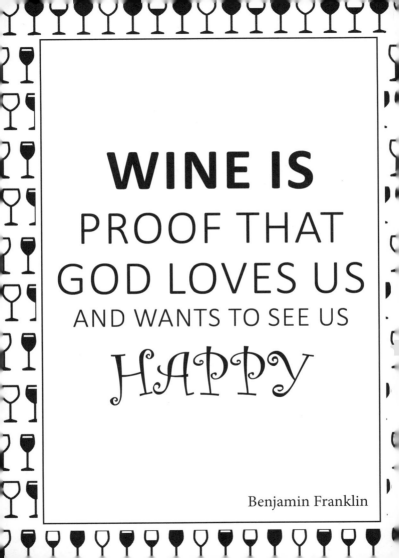

WINE IS
PROOF THAT
GOD LOVES US
AND WANTS TO SEE US
HAPPY

Benjamin Franklin

I love everything that's old...
old friends
old times
old manners
old books
old wine

Oliver Goldsmith

I cook with wine

Sometimes I even

add it to the food

W.C Fields

Let us
celebrate
the

occasion

with

WINE
and sweet words

You can't buy happiness but you can buy wine and that's kind of the same thing

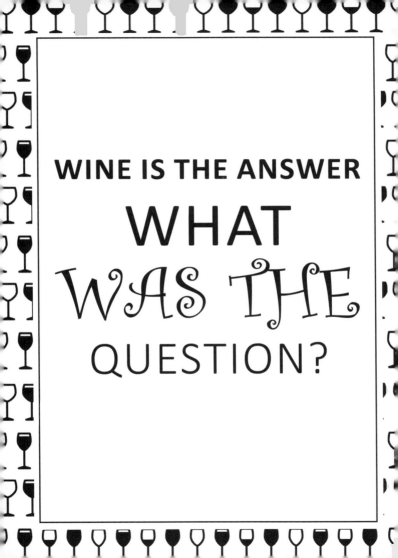

sorrow

can be alleviated by

a good sleep, a bath

and a glass of wine

Tomas Aquinas

Wine

is bottled poetry

Robert Louis Stevenson

It was so windy
that when I was
WALKING INTO
THE GYM
I got blown

into the

wine shop

We are all mortal until the first kiss and the second glass of wine

Eduardo Galeano

I MAKE WINE DISAPPEAR WHAT'S YOUR SUPER POWER?

To take wine into our mouths is to savor a droplet of human *history*

Clifton Fadiman

*The best wines are
the ones we drink
with friends*

Age and glasses of

wine

should never be

COUNTED

Italian proverb

I enjoy long romantic walks down
the wine aisle

Lord give me

coffee

to change the things I can and

wine

to accept the things I can't

Every empty wine bottle is filled with stories

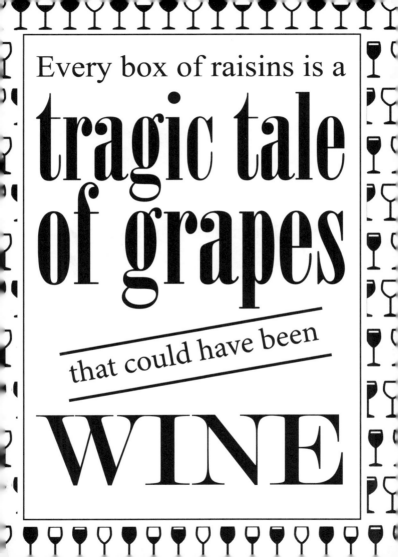

Every box of raisins is a
tragic tale of grapes
that could have been
WINE

Language is wine upon
the lips

Virginia Wolf

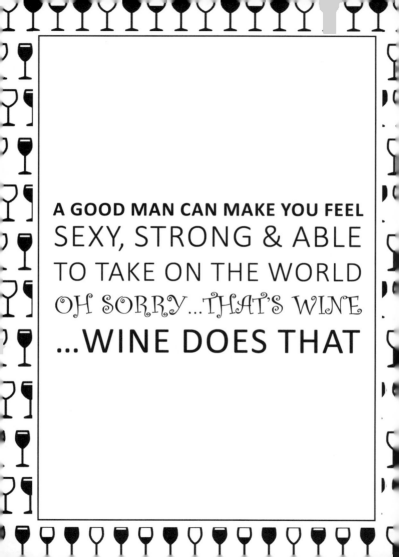

A GOOD MAN CAN MAKE YOU FEEL
SEXY, STRONG & ABLE
TO TAKE ON THE WORLD
OH SORRY...THAT'S WINE
...WINE DOES THAT

Wine is food and food is life and life is about the connections we make

Evan Dawson

For instant happy woman...
just add wine

People who say I'm hard to shop for clearly don't know where to buy *wine*

In wine there is truth

Ancient Roman proverb

Let's go wine tasting....
On the couch

Always keep a bottle
of wine in the fridge
for special occasions
You know...
Like Wednesday

Save water

Drink wine

I drink wine because I don't like to keep things bottled up

GIRLS
JUST WANNA HAVE
WINE

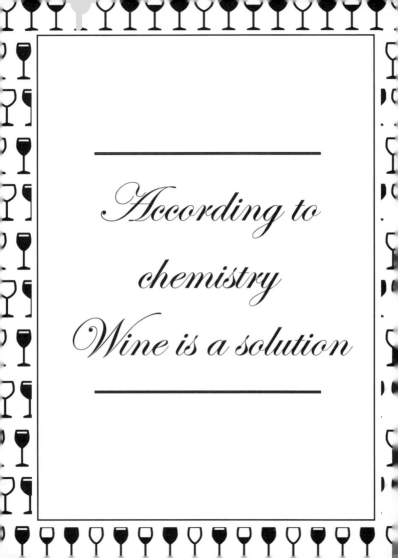

wine is

sunlight

held together by

WATER

Galileo Galilei

I'm a woman
I have needs
Pass me the wine

GOOD FOOD
GOOD WINE
GOOD FRIENDS
GOOD TIMES

I'VE GOT A MOUNTAIN OF
PROBLEMS
TO DEAL WITH SO I'M JUST GOING
TO HAVE SOME WINE AND
IGNORE THEM

Life is all the stuff you do between coffee time and wine time

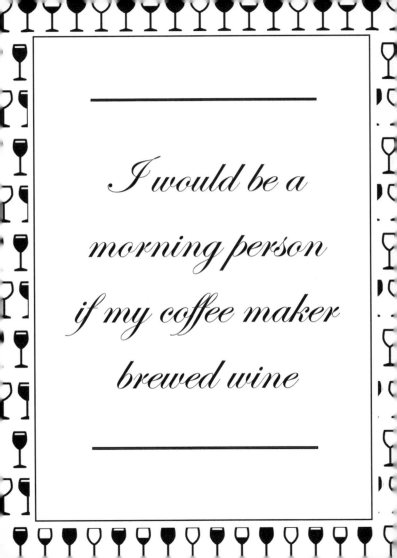

I would be a morning person if my coffee maker brewed wine

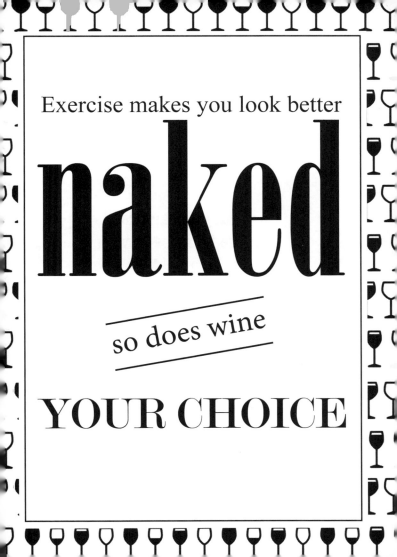

Yesterday I really really
wanted a glass of wine
Today I'm drinking wine
Always follow your dreams

WINE +
DINNER
=WINNER

TECHNOLOGY
WILL TRULY IMPRESS
ME THE DAY I CAN
DOWNLOAD
WINE

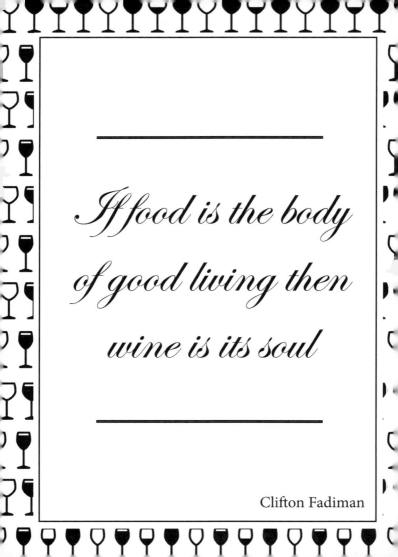

If food is the body of good living then wine is its soul

Clifton Fadiman

The secret to life is
pyjamas, wi-fi and wine

ADULTING
IS HARD
I DESERVE WINE

EVERYTHING

WILL BE JUST FINE

REMEMBER

TAKE LIFE ONE SIP AT A TIME